50
JOBS

WORSE
THAN
YOURS

Justin Racz

BLOOMSBURY

D0104567

Published by Bloomsbury, New York and London
Distributed to the trade by Holtzbrinck Publishers

All papers used by Bloomsbury are natural, recyclable products made
from wood grown in well-managed forests. The manufacturing processes conform to the
environmental regulations of the country of origin.

Library of Congress Cataloging-in-Publication Data

Racz, Justin.
50 jobs worse than yours / by Justin Racz.
p. cm.
Includes bibliographical references and index.
ISBN 1-58234-492-2
1. Occupations—Humor. I. Title: Fifty jobs worse than yours. II. Title.

PN6231.P74R33 2004
818'.5402—dc22

2004011182

First U.S. Edition 2004

7 9 10 8

Designed by Justin Racz and Elizabeth Van Itallie
Printed and bound in Singapore by Tien Wah Press

For my mother and brother, the best.

Job Listings

1. Sherpa
2. Afghani Travel Agent
3. "It's A Small World" Ride Operator
4. Chick Sexer
5. Saddam Hussein Double
6. Fast Food Condiment Prep Cook
7. Telemarketer
8. Cheesecake Tin Quality Control
9. Mop Duty
10. Garbage Barge Skipper
11. Roto-Rooterer Post–*Finding Nemo*
12. Rat Catcher
13. Data Entry
14. Telemarketing Scriptwriter
15. Spam Copywriter
16. B-List-Celebrity Assistant
17. Nursing Home Entertainer
18. Midget Tossing Tossee
19. Stevie Starr: Regurgitator
20. Maggot Wrangler
21. Adult-Video-Store Clerk
22. Walking Menu
23. Temp
24. Gas Station Foodmart Night Manager

25. Shopping Cart Valet
26. Singing Line Cook
27. Domino Setter-Upper
28. Pizza Delivery
29. Driver's Ed Instructor
30. Civil War Reenactor
31. Hazardous Materials Remover
32. NYC Taxi Driver
33. Torah Scribe
34. *Tush* Magazine Makeup Artist
35. Ratemyvomit.com Photo Editor
36. Gravedigger
37. The Before Guy
38. Exorcist
39. Tiruwka (Eastern European Highway Escort)
40. NYPD Harbor Unit: Body Recovery Detail
41. Cosmetics Tester
42. Thailand's Crocodile Hunter
43. Cellphone Salesperson
44. Little Boy Hand Model
45. Human Canvas
46. Office Plant-Watering Dude
47. Restaurant Bathroom Attendant
48. Neuroscience Technician
49. Airport Security Screener
50. Substitute Teacher
51. Your Job

1. Sherpa

THE JOB

Assist Mount Everest hikers with climbing, camp building, cooking, and schlepping.

SALARY

Base pay: $7 per day.

BONUS!

One dozen trips carrying five thousand pounds of tents, food, and oxygen canisters can earn a Sherpa the equivalent of four Frappuccinos.

FAME

International Sherpa celebrities include the late Babu Chhiri Sherpa of Takshindu and the attractive great but late Mrs. Pasang Lhama Sherpa of Surkye.
(Both died on expeditions.)

BENEFITS

Get a natural high at 27,000 feet.

DRAWBACKS

Freeze to death at 28,000 feet. (One out of twenty Sherpas doesn't make it to the next hike.)

2. Afghani Travel Agent

THE JOB

Offer exciting vacation packages at deep discounts to tourists.

DRESS CODE

Burka or chador for women; anything for men.

SKILLS

Be the best damn salesperson in the world.

SALARY

19,000 afghanis ($4) plus commission.

BENEFITS

Discounts on selected flights for friends and family. No blackout dates!

DRAWBACKS

Suggesting Americans sew Canadian flags onto their luggage and wear maple leaves.

3. "It's a Small World" Ride Operator

THE JOB

Escort children and parents into a motorized boat for an eleven-minute tour through the magical world of Disney: an international zip-a-dee-doo-dah spectacle featuring the sounds of the song the whole world sings.

EDUCATION

Training in amusement park safety and mechanical operation so as to prevent people from throwing themselves overboard.

SALARY

Employees, or "cast members" as Disney refers to them, can earn $10 an hour, but you have to work at the theme park for ten years first. Until then, $6.80.

SKILLS

Never let 'em see you frown: The mouse is all around.

BENEFITS

30 percent employee discount on all 30-percent-overpriced, parent-gouging merchandise.

DRAWBACKS

The chorus: "It's a small world after all."
Repeat 300 times a day x 7 hours a day x 5 days a week x 365 days a year.

4. Chick Sexer

THE JOB

The chick sexer looks for a penis. All male chicks have one, but so do 15 percent of females. In addition, the sexer examines the chickens' cloaca, the common external opening for the digestive, urinary, and reproductive tracts.

EDUCATION

The sign of a good sexer is his or her ability to distinguish the sex of females with penises. It requires keen observation, concentration, and a steady hand.

SALARY

$400 to $700 a day plus expenses.

HOURS

Nine to five. But it's nonstop. On average, a sexer sexes 5,000 to 7,000 chicks every day.

BENEFITS

Americans consume 6 billion chickens a year, the British 250 million. Without the chick sexer's role in fueling poultry production, there would be no All-U-Can-Eat wings and Rib Tips. Every Monday at Brother Jimmy's, NYC. Just $12.95!

DRAWBACKS

Getting more action at work than at home.

RECENTLY UNEMPLOYED

5. Saddam Hussein Double

THE JOB

Best described by a joke: An Iraqi general gathers all the Saddam doubles and tells them, "There's good news and bad news. The good news is you still have a job. The bombs the U.S. dropped did not kill our leader. The bad news is he lost an arm."

EDUCATION

Acting 201: Shakespearean tragedy.
Experience in major death scenes.

SALARY

Pretty good. Roughly $200 per day. However, that number is unconfirmed. (Unable to contact employee for verification.)

SKILLS

Near identical proportions of almost every body part of the former oppressor. A double must have an eye width of 5.34 cm. Truly.

BENEFITS

Look, feel, and often act like a ruler of 20 million.

DRAWBACKS

Look, feel, and act like a ruler of 20 million who's wanted dead by 3 billion.

6. Fast Food Condiment Prep Cook

THE JOB

The produce chopper is the backbone of every fast food restaurant. He or she is an invaluable cog in the burger, chicken, and fish sandwich–building machine.

ADVANCEMENT

Anywhere but down.

DRESS CODE

Smock, rubber gloves.

SALARY

$5.30 an hour, which is 15 cents better than minimum wage; no health plan; and one can be *asked* to work over forty hours without additional pay.

BENEFITS

Discarded lettuce heads and hour-old fries are always up for grabs.

DRAWBACKS

25 percent of the people in the U.S. will at one point in their lives have worked at McDonald's. Scary. Scarier still is sucking in fry grease all day and losing a digit.

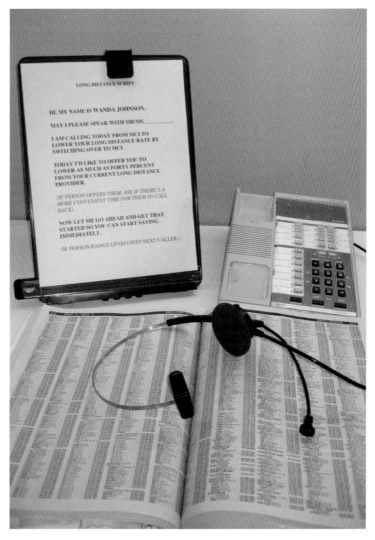

7. Telemarketer

THE JOB

Offer life insurance, credit card protection, 3-cent long-distance-calling plans, high school and college diplomas, loans, Omaha steaks, hearing aids, and bogus foreign lottery tickets.

HOURS

A.M. or P.M. eight-hour shift.

SALARY

$6 to $8 per hour plus commission.

DANGER

Being tracked down by a customer with outstanding caller-ID.

BENEFITS

Talk to people, briefly, from all over the world.

DRAWBACKS

When potential customers suggest you go have sex with yourself.

8. Cheesecake Tin Quality Control

Marks & Spencer Cheesecakes of London don't box themselves. And they definitely do not make sure that their tin lids are properly sealed. Such is the job of the cheesecake tin quality controller, who, 8,000 times an hour, gently applies pressure with a thumb making sure they are hermetically sealed.

Eight-hour day plus time-and-a-half thereafter.

2.50 pounds sterling per hour in 1991.
3.40 pounds sterling in 2004 adjusted for inflation.

Must have a Gandhi-like disposition so as not to lose it completely when cheesecake tin #382,839 comes down the line.

Free cake.

Numb thumb.

9. Mop Duty

THE JOB

Whether you've swabbed the deck on the U.S.S. *Midway* or the floor at McDonald's, you've tasted bitterness. The detail: Wake up at four A.M., arrive at the store by five, put the wet-floor sign out, fill the bucket with warm water and disinfectant, plunge, wring, mop, plunge, wring, mop until the wax tiles sparkle.

EDUCATION

Less is more. The more schooling one has, the lowlier the job feels. This is *the* entry-level job. There are no minimum education requirements.

SALARY

From minimum wage to $24,500 per year, though rarely does one last that long; the fast food industry has the highest employee turnover rate.

ADVANCEMENT

Condiment prep cook, fryer, assistant manager, manager, franchise owner, multifranchise owner, CEO, indicted CEO, minimum-security-prison mopper.

BENEFITS

Ronald also offers employees free meals up to $3.00. That's like three Big Macs. A nice perk for supersized HFFUs (Heavy Fast Food Users) with downsized pay.

DRAWBACKS

That piercing ammonia smell.

10. Garbage Barge Skipper

THE JOB

Pick up trash at dumps, motor, drop off at landfills.

DRESS CODE

Skipper hat, sunblock, deodorant.

SKILLS

No sense of smell. While street sanitation workers have walls dividing them and their haul, garbage barge skippers don't have that luxury.

TRAVEL

Garbage, it's everywhere you don't want to be. Wanderlusts, come aboard and journey to exotic lands like Paterson, New Jersey; Hempstead, New York; Ohio; and North Carolina. Long hauls will take take you to landfills in the Gulf of Mexico, the Bahamas, the Yucatán, Argentina . . .

BENEFITS

$12 per hour and up. Union benefits, collision insurance.

DRAWBACKS

In 1987, Duffy Saint Pierre set sail from Long Island City, New York, on the *Mobro 4000* with a 3,186-ton load. He was denied docking privileges at every port he attempted to enter — twelve over a stretch of three countries — and asked to move on. For 100 days straight he traveled until he returned the trash one mile from where he started: Long Island. "It's a stinking business," he said. Starboard side, port side, everywhere you look, crap's ahoy.

11. Roto-Rooterer
Post–*Finding Nemo*

THE JOB

Respond to calls from children who watched *Finding Nemo* and then set their fish "free" down the drain. Break it to them gently that Nemo ain't coming home.

EDUCATION

Training course in drain cleaning. Those seeking higher education attend the Roto-Rooter Plumbing School.

DRESS CODE

Blue oxford shirt, navy slacks, embroidered name tag.

SKILLS

A good bedside manner in order to explain that though their slogan is "Roto-Rooter, that's the name, and away go troubles down the drain," it doesn't apply to pets.

BENEFITS

The occasional miracle rescue. Roto-Rooterers have saved animals such as a pet parakeet, boa constrictor, tiger cub, puppies, and Teenage Mutant Ninja Turtles.

DRAWBACKS

Getting prank calls such as, "Can one of your guys come over and clean my pipes?" and "You guys suck."

Rat. It's what's for dinner.

12. Rat Catcher

THE JOB

Rat catcher ranks just below gravedigger (job #36), except in Bombay. According to municipal officials in India, over 20,000 residents, 40 percent of whom are university graduates, recently applied for seventy-one job vacancies.

HOURS

Day shift: Twelve to eight P.M. (day rat killer).
Night shift: Eight to four A.M. (night rat killer).

SALARY

For the princely sum of fifty-five rupees, or one British pound, all one has to do is catch twenty-five oversized bandicoot rats a night.

SKILLS

A nice, fluid baseball swing.

BENEFITS

Though it would eat into profits, caught vermin can make a nice dinner for two. Consider a light rat-tatouille appetizer. And for the second course, stuffed country rat in a wild mushroom sauce.

DRAWBACKS

Night rat killers of the Bombay Municipal Corporation (BMC) are often forced to take their rats home with them until the company's office opens the next day.

13. Data Entry

THE JOB

Enter names and addresses into a computer.

SKILLS

Typing; sight.

SALARY

$10 to $17 per hour in Manhattan.

TRAVEL

To the bathroom, snack machines, outside to grab a Parliament, and back.

BENEFITS

Be part of the exciting Information Age. Listen to music through headphones.

DRAWBACKS

Carpal-tunnel syndrome; neck, back, and eye strain; and mind numbing.

LONG DISTANCE SCRIPT

HI, MY NAME IS <u>WANDA JOHNSON.</u>

MAY I PLEASE SPEAK WITH MR/MS. _____?

I AM CALLING TODAY FROM _____ TO LOWER YOUR LONG DISTANCE RATE BY 50%.

(*IF PERSON INTERUPTS, JUST KEEP GOING*)

TODAY I'D LIKE TO OFFER YOU TO LOWER AS MUCH AS FORTY PERCENT FROM YOUR CURRENT LONG DISTANCE PROVIDER.

(*IF PERSON SAYS NO, JUST KEEP GOING.*)

NOW LET ME GO AHEAD AND GET THAT STARTED SO YOU CAN START SAVING IMMEDIATELY.

(*IF PERSON HANGS UP, CALL THEM BACK.*)

14. Telemarketing Scriptwriter

THE JOB

No matter how good or bad a product or service is, the sale is won or lost in the pitch. That's where you come in. Use your English major and tailor scripts to create a dialogue with the potential client then close the deal. ABC. *A*: Always. *B*: Be. *C*: Closing. *Always Be Closing.*

DRESS CODE

No reason to be presentable; no one sees you. If sales are good and the air conditioner is turned back on you'll need a lightweight cardigan.

SALARY

$30,000 per year, $50,000 if you're good.

SKILLS

"Telemarketing script development is an art." So says Outbound Telemarketing Company & Inbound Call Center Services. Use writing skills and neurolinguistic programming to strengthen the power of the message. *That's* what sells. *That's* the message.

BENEFITS

You're not a telemarketer.

DRAWBACKS

Scriptwriting hasn't helped your writing the way you had planned.

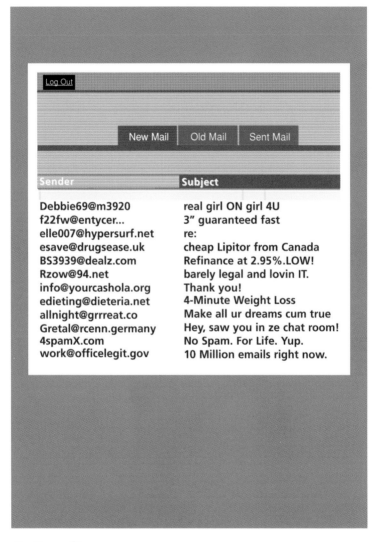

Log Out		
New Mail	Old Mail	Sent Mail

Sender	Subject
Debbie69@m3920	real girl ON girl 4U
f22fw@entycer...	3" guaranteed fast
elle007@hypersurf.net	re:
esave@drugsease.uk	cheap Lipitor from Canada
BS3939@dealz.com	Refinance at 2.95%.LOW!
Rzow@94.net	barely legal and lovin IT.
info@yourcashola.org	Thank you!
edieting@dieteria.net	4-Minute Weight Loss
allnight@grrreat.co	Make all ur dreams cum true
Gretal@rcenn.germany	Hey, saw you in ze chat room!
4spamX.com	No Spam. For Life. Yup.
work@officelegit.gov	10 Million emails right now.

15. Spammer

THE JOB

Write catchy and misleading e-mails with subject headings such as:
NEED A FEW INCHES? SHE'LL THANK YOU!
MORTGAGE RATES HIT ALL TIME LOW!
HI, IT'S JULIE AND I JUST GOT A WEBCAM!

EDUCATION

A loose grasp of the English language.

SALARY

$6 to $10 per hour.

SKILLS

A knack for playing into the reader's desires for deals and companionship.

BENEFITS

Your work is glanced over by millions of people every day.

DRAWBACKS

Admit Mom was right: You should have taken that civil service test.

DIANE PATRONE
B-List-Celebrity
Assistant

JOE NARCISO*
B-List Celebrity

16. B-List-Celebrity Assistant

*Joe's commercial, TV, and film credits: E*Trade and FedEx (lead roles); *Law and Order: Special Victims Unit* (Assistant Medical Examiner); *Third Watch* (Gary); *The Sopranos* (Richard); *A Good Night To Die* (Gun Salesman).

THE JOB

Tell your boss how absolutely great he/she is a few times a day. Log in what he/she wears every day so as not to repeat outfits for the phantom press; tell him/her how every other B-list celebrity is a washed-up hack — and ugly.

ADVANCEMENT

Working for a better celebrity.

SALARY

$30,000 plus party goody bags containing the latest magazine, a 50/50 cotton/polyester-blend T-shirt, the latest eyeliner, and complimentary scratch-paper cologne samples pour homme.

SKILLS

Suck up, be attractive, but not as attractive as B-list celebrity. If more attractive than celebrity, dress down and go easy on the makeup.

BENEFITS

Invites to B-list parties. Free top-shelf bar, the latest in hot hors d'oeuvres such as Peking duck wraps, chicken saté skewers, and tuna tartare on mini-toasts.

DRAWBACKS

Pick chickpeas out of celebrity's salad on command.

17. Nursing Home Entertainer

THE JOB

Perform humorous material in front of the geriatric.

ADVANCEMENT

The Catskills, universities, Stand-Up New York, Comic Strip Live, the Comedy Store, the Copacabana, Caesars Palace, HBO's *Def Comedy Jam*, Leno.

SALARY

$200 a set. Or for $2,000, a super-saver package deal of one show a month for twelve months.

SKILLS

Be loud.

BENEFITS

Even if you bomb, it will take the audience a long time to walk out.

DRAWBACKS

Hard to distinguish a laugh from a wheeze. And worse, you could kill.

18. Midget Tossing Tossee

THE JOB

Sell one's body for money. Though midget tossing is banned in the United States, Britain, and France, it's legal at Leopard's Lounge and Broil, Ontario, Canada. 5 percent discount if you mention this book.

DRESS CODE

Padded jacket, harness, helmet.

SALARY

Surprisingly good for a human projectile. A dwarf tossee who goes on tour can make a six-figure income.

FAME

The longest midget toss is said to have been made by an English truck driver, Jim Leonard. He tossed Lenny the Giant (4'4", 98 lbs.) eleven feet five inches. There is said to be an Australian record of thirty feet, but that is undocumented (formen.ign.com).

BENEFITS

Get a lot of attention from girls at bars.

DRAWBACKS

It's demeaning, according to the LPA (Little People of America): "Dwarfs are less participants in the sport than its object, like a football ball to a football match. What's special about tossing a dwarf? Why not a Jew toss, an African American toss, a woman toss, a dog toss?"

19. Stevie Starr: Regurgitator

THE JOB

Swallow foreign objects such as goldfish, needle and thread, a Rubik's Cube, and then bring them up whole, threaded, and solved.

EDUCATION

You can't teach this; it's a gift.

SKILLS

Complete command of your esophagus.

TRAVEL

Excite and appall audiences around the world.

BENEFITS

Get on David Letterman's "Stupid Human Tricks."

DRAWBACKS

Use your throat and stomach for purposes for which G-d didn't intend.

20. Maggot Wrangler

THE JOB

Handle larvae and put them on corpses in movies.

TRAVEL

Fly to set locations with a cooler full of unhatched flies.

SKILLS

Thick skin. One must not be squeamish or get emotionally attached to the little ones. (Maggots hatch on Wednesday and die on Friday.)

SALARY

$37 to $40 an hour.

BENEFITS

$37 to $40 an hour. Not bad for looking after larvae.

DRAWBACKS

Being called a maggot wrangler.

21. Adult-Video-Store Clerk

THE JOB

Rent and sell adult movies to those over eighteen; load and unload movies in the viewing kiosks; provide change for a dollar; clean up at the end of the day.

TRAVEL

Return *Deep Impacts, Ordinary Peepholes, Elephant Man, Girls Gone Hog Wild, BushWhacker II, Bare Naked in the Park, The Emperor Has No Clothes, Sopornos 5, Lip Service, Rearview Mila,* and *Happy Endings* to shelves.

SKILLS

Know if *Deep Impacts, Ordinary Peepholes, Elephant Man, Girls Gone Hog Wild, BushWhacker II, Bare Naked in the Park, The Emperor Has No Clothes, Sopornos 5, Lip Service, Rearview Mila,* and *Happy Endings* are in stock.

SALARY

Minimum wage plus free rentals and discounts on previously viewed titles.

BENEFITS

Autodidact Quentin Tarantino began his film career working as a video clerk, learning by watching. The adult film industry is a $100 billion industry and welcomes fresh talent and ideas. *Pulp Friction*?

DRAWBACKS

Being recognized by your minister.

22. Walking Menu

THE JOB

Walk among the restaurant's customers and present them with select illustrated items from the menu you're wearing.

DRESS CODE

A menu.

SKILLS

Look good in a menu.

FAME

Does anyone else have this job?

BENEFITS

Special discounts on ribs, Mexican salads, and lean bison burgers from the new Atkins menu.

DRAWBACKS

When customers ask you to turn around so they can look if you have anything good on the other side.

23. Temp

THE JOB

Play computer solitaire, Klondike, Snood; do the crossword; IM; take advantage of free long distance; call everyone you know; answer phones; conference-call friends; draft letters; create basic spreadsheets; Xerox; enter data; sneak out when an open-call acting audition comes up.

ADVANCEMENT

The coveted temp-to-perm position. If a temp is good, employers may dangle in front of them a full-time job with health benefits. But that pays less than working by the hour.

SALARY

Minimum wage, all the way to $25 an hour if you assist a CEO. Also, the more computer programs you know, the more temp agencies can bill you out for. Temps also have access to the supply closet . . .

SKILLS

Temp agencies require an exam which tests WPM (words per minute) and knowledge of Microsoft Office —Word, Excel, PowerPoint, Outlook.

BENEFITS

The temp job doubles as a writer's home office. This is where novels, screenplays, and books about bad jobs are written.

DRAWBACKS

All the free time one has to contemplate life's bigger questions: *Why am I here? What am I going to do with my life? I have no girlfriend. My friends are all getting engaged. Am I depressed? Should I go on this Paxil? My hair's falling into the keyboard. Was Grandpa bald?*

24. Gas Station Foodmart Night Manager

THE JOB

Deter robbery. Know when to remove bad milk and skunked beer. Refill the cheesefood in the nacho cheese machine.

EDUCATION

N/A.

SALARY

Minimum wage up to $10.25 an hour.

SKILLS

Be cool. Earn the respect of the skater punks and they will not steal your Red Bull.

BENEFITS

Free food, free Slushies, free rein of the porno mags as long as you are in a security camera blind spot.

DRAWBACKS

As Middle East relations with the U.S. and England worsen, robbers are keenly aware that a restriction of foreign oil production will send gasoline prices higher, creating a surplus of cash in register drawers.

25. Shopping Cart Valet

THE JOB

Collect shopping carts from the parking lot and put them back in front of the store.

HOURS

Nine A.M. to when the last cart is collected and neatly arranged for the next day's shoppers. This can take the parking lot valet until after ten P.M. in a quiet, big, dark, and scary lot, alone.

DRESS CODE

Khaki shorts, jogging shoes, tucked-in golf shirt, orange reflective tank top.

SALARY

$10 per hour Monday to Friday. $12 weekends.

BENEFITS

Sometimes get to drive the golf cart when it's rigged. With twenty-five carts and you're cruising at 5 mph, there's nothing like bringing in a herd.

DRAWBACKS

Carts crippled by SUVs must be taken out back and shot.

This photo is a representation of a singing line cook. He is not a Lick's employee.

26. Singing Line Cook

THE JOB

Assemble burgers and sing happy songs at superfun restaurants, such as Lick's, home of the Homeburg. Apply now and soon you can sing the Homeburg song to the tune of the *Flintstones* theme: *Homeburg, have a homeburg! Have a homeburger and golden fri-i-ies!*

FAME

Before *American Idol*, restaurants with singing staff were the platform for superstardom. Hip-hopper Sisqo started out at The Fudgery, singing "The Fudge Song" while making fudge before customers at the mall.

DRESS CODE

T-shirt emblazoned with **I ♥ LICK'S**. When cheesy and greasy uniform becomes Febreze-resistant, employees must buy a new one from the company store.

SALARY

$6.75 Canadian per hour (in 1996). Bonuses are tied to a color star system. Gold star = perfect. Silver = very good. Red = average. Green . . . Well, no one gets a green star, unless you go and shoot up the place.

BENEFITS

There's a chance the vice president of Jive Records is waiting in line and listening to you sing.

DRAWBACKS

There's a chance the vice president of Jive Records is waiting in line and listening to you sing.

27. Domino Setter-Upper

THE JOB

Set up dominoes one after another on your hands and knees. Design them into patterns and logos.

DRESS CODE

Knee pads.

SALARY

$60 for children's birthday parties.

TOOLS

Yardstick, domino stoppers, Scotch tape.

BENEFITS

The tremendous satisfaction of seeing it work at the end.

DRAWBACKS

The tremendous disappointment of seeing it not work; kids crying; parents demanding a refund.

28. Pizza Delivery

THE JOB

Deliver pizzas.

TRAVEL

On an average night a driver travels 75 to 100 miles, or roughly 25,000 miles a year. Drivers use their own car and must refill the gas tank at their own expense.

EDUCATION

Driver's license.

SALARY

Mostly tips or lack thereof. Cash tips can range from nothing to discontinued foreign coins mixed in with loose change. Noncash tips include verbal tips such as thank-yous, religious blessings, and holiday wishes.

BENEFITS

Delivering to college campuses can have its perks. In lieu of a cash tip, one can get paid in bong hits and loose buds.

DRAWBACKS

The number one most dangerous job for college students! Dangers include muggings on the way from the curb to the front door; carjacking; getting robbed and shot. Pizza joints also don't offer life insurance.

29. Driver's Ed Instructor

THE JOB

Those who can't do, teach. Those who can't teach, teach gym. And those who can't teach gym put their lives and a combustion engine in the hands of hormone-imbalanced teenagers, four times a week after school.

DRESS CODE

Something incredibly lame. Button-down short-sleeve shirt, slacks, white socks, black sneaker-shoes.

SALARY

It's not for the money. It's for the children.

TRAVEL

In and out of parking spaces; 25 mph in a 40 mph zone. Never, never on the highway.

BENEFITS

Screening the propaganda film *Red Asphalt 3* for your students and scaring the living daylights out of them. A cult classic, the educational film replete with gratuitous gore, death, and dismemberment strongly motivates young drivers to avoid moving violations.

DRAWBACKS

80 percent of all accidents involve drivers under the age of eighteen.

30. Civil War Reenactor

THE JOB

Act in the grand theater of the Civil War. Replay the great battles such as Fredericksburg, Harpers Ferry, Antietam, six days a week. Wake up at five A.M., beat a drum, sing rally songs, fire a musket, play the fife, drop dead.

DRESS CODE

40-pound wool U.S. overcoat for infantry ($145); U.S. enlisted frockcoat ($130); military vest ($46); Confederate officer double-breasted shell jacket ($45); getting stabbed in the chest with a plastic bayonet, priceless.

TOOLS

Fifes aren't cheap: $55 for a nineteenth-century reproduction. As well, canteen, brogans (shoes), musket (with bayonet and scabbard), Colt 1860, mess kit, underwear.

ADVANCEMENT

One day you could be a fake general.

BENEFITS

Live out the South's antebellum dream of bringing down the Union.

DRAWBACKS

No ROTC program.

31. Hazardous Materials Remover

THE JOB

Identify, remove, pack, transport, and dispose of hazardous materials, including asbestos, lead-based paint, and radioactive materials.

EDUCATION

Specialized training and certification in hazardous waste management.

SALARY

$11.09 per hour, $21,030 to $53,430 per year.

SKILLS

Operate earth-moving equipment or trucks; chemical-spill experience a plus.

BENEFITS

Great training for *Fear Factor*.

DRAWBACKS

Your wife won't touch you until you've showered after work for a good forty-five minutes.

32. NYC Taxi Driver

THE JOB

Drive, honk, pick up fares. Repeat.

EDUCATION

Driver's license.

SALARY

$75 per day, $20,000 per year.

SKILLS

Offensive driving. Speaking English helps, but is not necessary. Nine out of ten new drivers are immigrants from eighty-four countries, including Pakistan, India, Iraq, Iran, Egypt, and republics of the former USSR.

BENEFITS

The dubious honor of having the most dangerous job in New York City; complete control of the radio; and the right of way.

DRAWBACKS

No compensation.
No social security.
No disability.
No health insurance.
Nothing but the right of way.

33. Torah Scribe

THE JOB

The job of a sofer, or Torah Scribe, is to write and repair Torah scrolls by hand: 248 columns, 80 parchment pages, for a total of 304,805 individual Hebrew letters. It can take a full day to do one column, a third of a Torah page, and up to one year to complete an entire Torah.

TOOLS

No Wite-Out. The Torah is considered a living document and must be made entirely of natural materials such as kosher ink made from the crushed outer bark of a wasp's nest, a quill made from a turkey or goose feather, and cloth made from a calf killed for food.

SALARY

Salaries depend on the price a sofer charges for a scroll. Prices may vary.
Israel: 24K to 26K per scroll.
U.S.: 30K to 36K.
U.S. Northeast: 40K to 60K.

SKILLS

The patience of a prophet and great handwriting.

BENEFITS

To be a Torah scribe is to write yourself into the 5,765-year history of the chosen people.

DRAWBACKS

You can't spell-check this document. If just one letter is incorrect or missing, the Torah is considered no good.

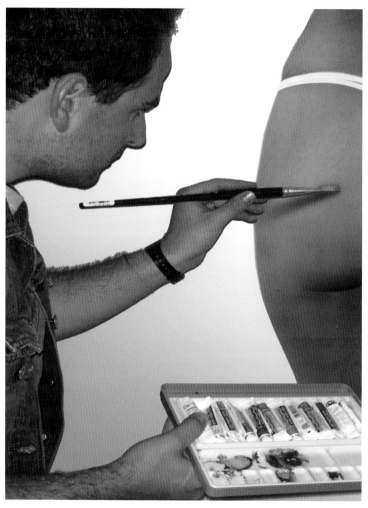

34. *Tush* Magazine Makeup Artist

Apply a series of foundations and toners to alter and enhance a derriere's complexion.

"Must have a good knowledge of the products they use and how to apply them. They must know about the latest styles and colours, and be familiar with their clients' requirements." (www.KiwiCareers.govt.nz.)

On-staff *Tush* makeup artists earn anywhere from $45,000 to $60,000 a year. Freelancers get a day rate of $300 and up, depending on their experience and responsibilities such as number of asses being made up.

People skills, artistic ability, and an eye for color.

Get to work up close with minor celebrities.

It's not *Face* magazine.

35. Ratemyvomit.com Photo Editor

THE JOB

Ensure that no inappropriate or offensive pictures or comments are posted on the site. For example, if someone posts a picture of their pet vomiting, should it go up? What about plastic vomit? Would the purists object?

DRESS CODE

Boxer shorts and socks, just like everyone else working on the Net.

SALARY

Compensation is based on a profit-sharing plan. In other words, zero. But the site is constantly expanding its fan base and when advertisers jump on board, that's when the real money starts coming in.

FAME

The content editor is now considered cool by his little brother and his friends because they heard Howard Stern on the radio talking about the site.

TRAVEL

See foods from all over the world.

DRAWBACKS

You work in the medium of retch.

36. Gravedigger

THE JOB

Dig. Then dig some more. And when the grass grows over the grave, mow. Then mow some more.

HOURS

There's a reason it's called the graveyard shift. Many workers wait until dusk to dig so as not to disrupt services going on during the day.

SALARY

$15 to $350 per grave depending on the cemetery. However, the Clark's Cemetery believes gravedigging is less a job than a joy. Here's their offer: Donate just $25 and it's All-U-Can-Dig at Clark's. Open 24 hours! Send check or money order to: VFW Post 2485, Grave Diggers, Box R-CV, FPO AP 96517.

SKILLS

A strong back; a strong stomach.

BENEFITS

Ten thousand people die a day, so there's always work. Also, many cemeteries offer worker incentives, such as a friends-and-family discount on plots and headstones.

DRAWBACKS

DBO (Dead Body Odor). True story: One gravedigger literally dug his own grave when his pick struck through a coffin lid. The grave emitted a dreadful effluvium that triggered arrhythmic breaths, convulsions, and his sudden death.

WANT MUSCLE?

BEFORE

AFTER

37. The Before Guy

38. Exorcist

THE JOB

Stand in front of a camera for an FDA-unapproved fast-weight-loss and muscle-gain product; vaguely resemble the After guy; be balding and/or fat. Have a Buddha belly.

ADVANCEMENT

The After guy.

SALARY

$50 AFTRA union wage or negotiated fee. Residuals from infomercials.

HOURS

Minutes or up to a full day of shooting.

BENEFITS

See yourself in print and on TV.

DRAWBACKS

Be recognized in print and on TV.

39. Tiruwka
(Eastern European Highway Escort)

THE JOB

Issue the commands of G-d against a force of evil to drive out the devil from the possessed.

EDUCATION

Formal training in exorcism rituals, such as purification and evil voice detection.

SALARY

"You cannot serve both G-d and money." (Matthew 6:24–34).

TOOLS

Salt (symbolizing purity), wine (symbolizing the blood of Christ), a crucifix, the Bible, and holy water.

BENEFITS

A ticket to heaven.

DRAWBACKS

Green bile stains.

THE JOB

Stand on the side of the highway and flag down those looking for a little company.

EDUCATION

From none to an engineering degree. Highway hooking is always an optional fall (on your) back profession.

DRESS CODE

Thigh-highs, galoshes, umbrella for inclement Polish weather. Because the casually dressed Tiruwka is often mistaken for a hitchhiker, it is important that she wear as little as possible and dye her brightly.

ADVANCEMENT

Tiruwka is your basic one-star hooker. The next rung up is streetwalker, then brothel whore, and the crême de la hook, the escort with management.

BENEFITS

Be your own boss, work outdoors, meet interesting people.

DRAWBACKS

Services rendered in cabs of trucks often lead to severe back and neck injury.

40. NYPD Harbor Unit: Body Recovery Detail

THE JOB

Dive into forty-degree water three times a day to recover bodies, parts of bodies, and key pieces of evidence.

DRESS CODE

Dry suit, oxygen, towel, change of clothes.

SALARY

$45,000 per year. Full pension after twenty years of service.

TRAVEL

The Harlem River, Hudson River, city reservoir, and any other body of water that touches any of the five boroughs of New York City.

BENEFITS

Help solve crime.

DRAWBACKS

It's not exactly diving at the Great Barrier Reef in Australia. No fish, just those sleeping with them.

41. Cosmetic Tester

THE JOB

While this opportunity is not open to British rabbits (the UK has stopped all animal testing for finished cosmetics), U.S. rabbits can easily find employment in the field of cosmetic research. Specific duties include being shaved, poked, prodded, and probed.

EDUCATION

N/A.

ADVANCEMENT

Pet rabbit, a rabbit in a hat, Bugs Bunny, or the Trix rabbit.

SALARY

Vitamin drops, carrots.

BENEFITS

In the event that hell freezes over and as a result humans evolve to grow a warm, furry coat, we will know which mascara and blush are safe to use.

DRAWBACKS

Eye irritation, swelling, reddening, blindness, rashes, hives, bleeding, ulceration. Mild to intense pain; dizziness; hair-thinning; pink paw.

42. Thailand's Crocodile Hunter

THE JOB

Warm up the crowd by wedging your head into the crocodile's jaw so it can't clamp down. Follow up with a big number like reaching into its gullet, retrieving a touch of bile, then tasting it, to the audience's delight.

DRESS CODE

Michael Jackson's outfit from "Thriller."

SALARY

100 baht, or about $2.50.

HOURS

Five shows a day in downtown Pattaya.

BENEFITS

Steve Irwin has nothing on this guy. Steve would have to shove his son inside a croc's mouth to match Thailand's croc master.

DRAWBACKS

Five helpings of bile a day can't be healthy.

43. Cellphone Salesperson

THE JOB

Stand outside wireless store. Hand out fliers for free phones with two-year contract. Be enthusiastic.

DRESS CODE

Inflatable cellphone. Underneath the costume, it's your call. Shorts and a T-shirt in the summer. Think thermals in the winter.

SALARY

$8 per hour. Time and a half after thirty-five hours.

DANGER

Being approached by a child and getting punched in the zero.

BENEFITS

No one knows it's you in there.

DRAWBACKS

Your next job is playing a taco.

Sasha Eden

44. Little Boy Hand Model

THE JOB

Sasha Eden has just what the toy-truck companies and commercial directors are looking for: small hands and a long attention span.

HOURS

Yes, a seven-year-old would seem the natural choice to show off a seven-year-old's hand playing with Truckasaurus or Tickle-Me Elmo. But a twenty-five-year-old is less likely to pee her pants after being verbally abused by the director for the shape her cuticles are in.

SALARY

$100 per hour for a good hand job.

FAME

Famous appendages include the finger that pushes in the stomach of the Pillsbury Doughboy and the hand that pulls a cheesy slice from a Pizza Hut Stuffed Crust pizza.

BENEFITS

$100 per hour to do puppetry? It almost makes it worth it not being able to palm a grapefruit.

DRAWBACKS

Being on a shoot where a little boy compares recent credits and brags that he just played opposite DeNiro.

45. Human Canvas

46. Office Plant-Watering Dude

THE JOB

Let strangers paint you to raise money for the Little Missionary's Day Nursery School in Manhattan.

TOOLS

Paintbrush, quarts of $2 paint from Kmart, your Sunday worst, your body.

SALARY

$1 per paint job. $150 per day. Because it's a cash business, it's not hard to skim off the top.

DANGER

Don't smoke, you're flammable.

BENEFITS

You're also vulnerable. Women find that sexy.

DRAWBACKS

If you're in a gang, being a human canvas is not good for your street cred.

47. Restaurant Bathroom Attendant

THE JOB

Every week go to fifty company offices, water the plants, manicure the leaves, massage the soil.

DRESS CODE

It's hard to pick up secretaries when you have a pink feather duster in your back pocket.

SALARY

$11 per hour plus medical. Overtime after forty hours.

ADVANCEMENT

No.

BENEFITS

Good stories. One office plant waterer was making the rounds in the lobby of the offices of an afternoon talk show where he found a carving knife sticking out of the topsoil.

DRAWBACKS

Plants far from the men's room smell vaguely of pee.

THE JOB

Turn on faucet, turn off faucet; hand towels to clients; offer refreshments from the custodial buffet, such as breath mints and cologne; tidy up sink and stalls.

EDUCATION

N/A.

SALARY

Cash tips.

ADVANCEMENT

The coat-check girl.

DRESS CODE

Black tie.

DRAWBACKS

While you work the clientele thinks, "Yeah, why don't I come over to your house and watch you take a leak? You think you're getting a few pennies because you passed me a towel? Wanker."

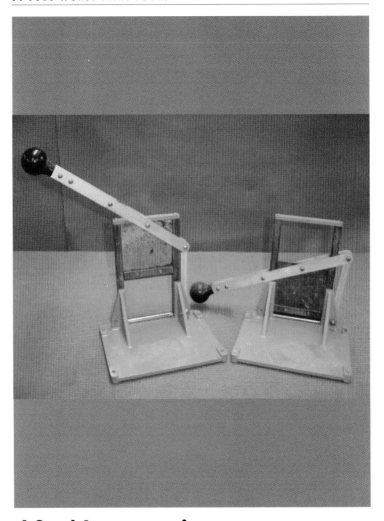

48. Neuroscience Technician

THE JOB

Cut off heads of baby rats, mice, other rodents, and birds for neuroscience medical research.

SKILLS

Being good with the Decapitator.
Product #462003 at www.myNeuroLab.com.

SALARY

In smaller university labs entry-level technicians make roughly $25,000.

ADVANCEMENT

Decapitator is the mailroom position of the medical industry. Neurosurgery is about twenty-one rungs north. Chief of Staff, 104.

DANGER

Losing a pinky.

DRAWBACKS

Cadaver decapitator. (It requires a bone saw.)

49. Airport Security Screener

Be part of America's Homeland Security Program by using the latest in electronic imaging and frisking technology.

You must be a U.S. citizen or a U.S. national; have a high school diploma, GED, or equivalent or at least one year of full-time work experience in security work, aviation screener work, or as an x-ray technician.

Now that screeners are federal employees, they receive a good wage: $23,600 to $35,400, plus health insurance, retirement benefits, and paid leave. Private-sector screeners earn minimum wage, or around $10,000 a year.

Rubber gloves, that electro wand.

Feel up a passenger without having to take him or her out to dinner and a movie.

Any hard object seems suspicious.

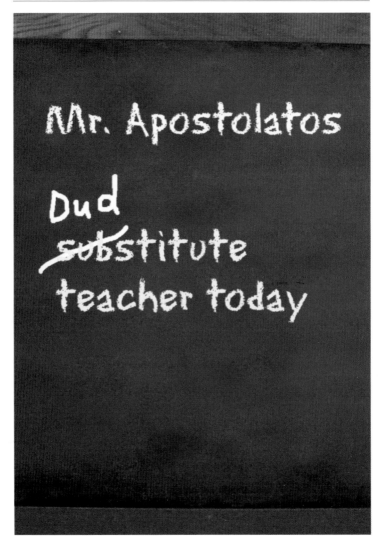

50. Substitute Teacher

THE JOB

Take roll call. That will take twenty minutes. Watch your students have a field day with you: One kid pretends not to speak English; two switch names; a third snitches on a popular girl cutting class. And the note passing? Forget about it.

EDUCATION

Loose knowledge of the three R's: reading, writing, and arithmetic.

SALARY

Private school: $100 per day.
Public school: $50 per day. But the institutional mac & cheese and quarter pint of milk is just $1.25.

TOOLS

Chalk, ruler, protractor, paddle.

BENEFITS

School of Rock starring Jack Black helped the image of the sub immeasurably.

DRAWBACKS

Sneak your class out of school to a rock concert and you'll need Johnnie Cochran by noon.

51. Your Job

THE PHOTOGRAPHERS:

"It's a Small World" Ride Operator: Edward Chapman
Chick Sexer: Corbis
Saddam Hussein Double: Jim Hollander, courtesy of EPA
Cheesecake Tin Quality Control: Billy Siegrist
Rat Catcher: Michael Freeman/Corbis
Garbage Barge Skipper: Todd A. Gipstein/Corbis
Sherpa: David Kelly
Midget Tossing Tossee: Courtesy of Al Fields
Roto-Rooterer: Courtesy of Paul Abrams, Roto-Rooter
Bunny: Chris Collins/Corbis
Stevie Starr, Regurgitator: Courtesy of Mike Malley Entertainment
Maggot Wrangler: David Meyers
Domino Setter-Upper: Courtesy of Scott Suko
Pizza Delivery Guy: Courtesy of Henry Burross
Civil War Reenactor: Peter Guttman/Corbis
Hazardous Material Remover: Eric Van Skyhawk
Torah Scribe: Bill Aron
Vomit Guy: Courtesy of Joe Lipson
Gravedigger: Vince Sabatini
Tush Makeup Artist, Substitute Teacher: Julie Soefer
The Tush: Christopher Fragapane
Thailand's Crocodile Hunter: Hin Or
Decapitator: Courtesy of myNeuroLab.com
Little Boy Hand Model: Joel Markman, Julie Soefer
Right and left thumb, plus retouching: Eric Van Skyhawk
All other photographs by Justin Racz

THE PHOTOGRAPHED:

Afghani Travel Agent: Melinda Ward
Rat Catcher: Ramon
B-List-Celebrity Assistant: Diane Patrone
B-List Celebrity: Joe Narciso
Nursing Home Entertainer: David Johnson
Temp: Catherine Gionfriddo
Walking Menu: Felix
Singing Line Cook: Courtesy of Dojo, New York City
Domino Setter-Upper: Scott Suko, Dominotoppling.com
Maggot Wrangler: Marissa Schwierjohn
Pizza Delivery Guy: Gary, from Foiled: the movie. foiled.uk
Civil War Reenactor: Unknown
NYC Taxi Driver: Clarence Cook
Torah Scribe: Rabbi Miller
Vomit Guy: Jiten D. Parmar
Data Entry Keyer: Meira Cohen
Exorcist: Mitch Bennett
Before and After: Sherrod, Enzo, Sean K.
Gravedigger: Harold Horton
Tush: Chastity
Bathroom Attendant: Alec Brownstien; patron: Jason Hoff
Office Plant-Watering Dude: Todd James; executive: Thompson Harrell
Little Boy Hand Model: Sasha Eden
Substitute Teacher: Rebeka Racz and friends

I'd like to thank my agent, Betsy Lerner,
for making my day once again; and to everyone
at Bloomsbury and the Gernert Company.
Many happy returns.

Thank You:

Nicholas Apostolatos
George Brewington
Josh Cahill
Crewcuts
DTUT, my office
Ryan D'Agostino
Dave the Dwarf
Mario H. Denis
Colin Dickerman
Al Fields
Maciej Flisak
Rachel Frankle
Alona Fryman
Panio Gianopoulos

Yelena Gitlin
Naomi Horne
Adam Kantor
Betsy Lerner
Sarah London
Shara Mendelson
Scott Mitnick
Marisa Pagano
Mish Perfilov
Ellen K. Racz
Greg Racz
Rebeka Racz
Brian Rea
Danny Roth

Karen Rudnicki
Vince Sabatini
Rachel Salomon
Melissa Schwierjohn
Adam Silver of
  Strengthnet
Julie Soefer
Jason Tandon
Mary Tucker
Peter Tucker
Elizabeth Van Itallie
Enzo Velazquez
Martin Wierzbicki

SOURCES:

1. Grossman, Kari Grady. "The Ice Doctors," Discovery.com, April 2002
    Sherpa Friendship Association
    photo: www.dungevalley.co.uk, for all your British plant and garden needs.

3. "The Facts: The House of the Mouse," *The New Internationalist*, 2000,
    www.newint.org/issue308/facts
    "Working at Disney World: It's No Fun," *The New Internationalist*
    Ellwood, Wayne. "Inside the Disney Dream Machine" and "Service with a Smile"
    The New Internationalist, December 1998

4. McGrory, Linda. "Can't Find a Good Chicken Sexer? Just Ask." *Irish Examiner*, 2000
    Martin, R.D. *The Specialist Chick Sexer*. Melbourne: Bernal Publishing, 1994

5. Sloan, Sam."The Many Faces of Saddam Hussein," 2002
    www.ishipress.com/saddams.htm

8. Jon Arnold, former Marks & Spencer employee, 1991

10. Abadjian, Nick, and Richard Schack. "Garbage: Queens' Trashy Tale," *Queens Tribune.* 2001

11. Paul Abrams, Public Relations, Roto-Rooter Services Company

12. "Rat Catcher," *Irish Times*, City Edition, 1996
    www.terrierman.com/indiachi.htm

14. 5 Star Outbound Telemarketing Company & Inbound Call Center Services
    www.5star-telemarketing.com/telemarketing-scripts

17. Interview with Harley Scheck, 2003

18. Photo: Dave the Dwarf. Represented by Al Fields
    "Trippy Tryptic: For the Dwarf in All of Us," IGN for Men; www.formen.ign.com/news

19. Mike Malley Entertainments, mikemalley@ukstars.co.uk

20. Interview with Jim Brockett, Brockett's Film Fauna, 2003

24. Taylor, Aaron. "Convenience Store Blues," www.jobstories.com/stories/taylor.htm
    National Association of Convenience Stores, NACS online

26. Anonymous. "Lick's Sucks!"
    www.geocities.com/SoHo/Den/3001/dofferings/licks.html
    Interview with Beau Levitt, former Lick's employee

28. APDD (Association of Pizza Delivery Drivers)
www.pizzadeliverydrivers.com
"What delivering pizza does to our cars," www.tipthepizzaguy.com, 2001
Photo featured in *Foiled*, the movie. www.foiled.co.uk

29. South, Carol. "Cruise Control." Grand Traverse *Herald*
Brandenburg, Melissa. "Films Create Scared Drivers." *Albuquerque Journal*. October 2003

30. Interview with Richard Lewis of Pamplin Historical Park & The National Museum of the Civil War Soldier. Petersburg, Virginia, 2003
civilwarsaga.homestead.com; cwreenactors.com/faqj

31. U.S. Bureau of Labor Statistics

32. Schaller, Bruce. *New York City Taxicab Fact Book*, 3rd Edition. September 2003
NYC Taxi and Limousine Commission, www.schallerconsult.com/taxi

33. Osgood, Charles. The Osgood File (CBS Radio Network): 9/12/02
www.torahscribe.com; Rabbi Miller; Neal Yerman, Torah Scribe.

34. *Tush* magazine is a pseudonym for a butt focused publication

35. Joe Lipson, Ratemyvomit.com creator and editor

36. Rana-Baradas Master Sgt. Louis. "Be a Grave Digger" *Airman: The Magazine of America's Air Force*, 2002
Downing, Catherine. "Grave Digger: A Shovel, a Pickax and Some Tough Bones." *The Anniston Star*, 2003.

38. Catholic Encyclopedia: Exorcism, *New Advent*, www.newadvent.org.cathen

39. Interview with Helene

40. "Dealing with the Stress of Recovering Human Dead Bodies." USACHPPM: Readiness through Health.

44. AAVS: American Anti-Vivisection Society; worldanimal.net

   Other job information provided by the U.S Bureau of Labor Statistics

A Note on the Author

Justin Racz is an advertising copywriter.
His parody, *J.Crewd*, was published in 1998.
He lives in New York City.